Kingdom *Kidz* Bible

with envelope surprises!

Martha and Mary

Luke10:38–42

PROMISE
PRESS

An Imprint of Barbour Publishing

Jesus came to visit their house! Mary and Martha were so excited. They knew Jesus was their special Friend. They believed Jesus was the Son of God. Jesus was here to visit!

S crub, scrub, scrub. Martha cleaned the table.
Swish, swoosh, swoosh.

Martha swept the floor. Jesus was here to visit!

Mary sat at Jesus' feet, listening to every word He said. She listened and listened, learning more about God. Jesus was here to visit!

Chop, chop, chop. Martha fixed the food. Splish, splash, splish. Martha washed the dishes. Jesus was here to visit!

Mary still sat at Jesus' feet, listening to His words about God. Suddenly Martha stopped cooking and cleaning.

"Jesus!" Martha cried. "I'm doing all the work! Tell my sister Mary to come and help me."

M artha, Jesus said with a smile. "Mary has discovered how important it is to spend time with Me, learning about God. Stop being busy for awhile. Come sit here beside Mary. I want you to spend time with Me, too."

I like to spend time with Jesus. Today I pray,
Dear Jesus, help me remember to spend time with You every day. Amen.

I know it's important to spend time with Jesus and with God. The Bible tells me how Jesus spent time with God, too. Here's a verse that tells me what Jesus did.

"[Jesus] went up on a mountainside to pray." MARK 6:46